LES PETITS PLATS
FRANÇAIS
SIMON & SCHUSTER
ILLUSTRATED

scrumptious muffins

MARC GROSSMAN

(alias Bob)

Photography by Akiko Ida
Styling by Sophie Glasser

SIMON &
SCHUSTER
ILLUSTRATED

London · New York · Sydney · Toronto

A CBS COMPANY

English language edition published in Great Britain by
Simon & Schuster UK Ltd, 2011
A CBS Company

Copyright © Marabout 2008

SIMON AND SCHUSTER ILLUSTRATED BOOKS
Simon & Schuster UK
222 Gray's Inn Road
London WC1X 8HB
www.simonandschuster.co.uk

1 2 3 4 5 6 7 8 9 10

Translation: Prudence Ivey
Copy editor English language: Nicki Lampon

Colour reproduction by Dot Gradations Ltd, UK
Printed and bound in U.A.E.

ISBN 978-0-85720-248-2

Contents

It's not easy to find a good muffin!

At the risk of sounding a bit narcissistic, I must say that I have never really liked muffins made by others.

I think we attach too much importance to their appearance. It's no good if they look great and smell delicious but, when you taste them, there's nothing there… just dry sponge with a sugary taste. 'Ah! Conned again!'

So, after years of bemoaning the difficult life of the muffin lover, I decided that it was time to do something. Instead of complaining, I would take action.

I had never taken a cooking course and I do not pretend to have an ounce of authority on the matter, but I know from experience that you must accept that you'll make mistakes.

In this book, I will show you my best muffin recipes. Muffins that aren't just good to look at. Muffins that are always good, each time you make them.

Advice from Bob

Socrates said: 'One must eat to live and not live to eat'. OK, but even so, I think it's stupid to make muffins that are healthy but that no one wants to eat. I think that food should be as healthy as possible without sacrificing pleasure. And I have often said that the ingredients that make my muffins healthy are the same as those that make people like them. Keeping this in mind, here's some information on ingredients that you may find useful.

Fruit

Everyone knows that eating lots of fruit is good for you. But the more a fruit is cooked, the more nutrients it loses. To alleviate this problem, I do the following: I cook the fruit at the centre of the muffin where the temperature rises least, and I use big pieces of fruit where possible to ensure they don't cook too much. I also use lots of fruit. Really a lot. As much as possible without the muffin collapsing. I tread the line between healthy and delicious!

Fat

I like butter – like most people. On toast, on pancakes, on potatoes, on pasta. I put butter on everything but I never use butter substitute products. That said, butter is not always the best ingredient for making muffins.

I often prefer sunflower oil. As well as being better for the heart, as a polyunsaturated fat (unlike butter, which is a saturated fat), it also makes really moist muffins. Vegetable oil mixes with flour better than butter and avoids producing too much gluten and drying out the muffin.

White or brown flour

Most recipes in this book use plain white flour. Unrefined, or wholewheat, flour is an excellent source of fibre, vitamins and minerals. Unfortunately, the majority of these nutrients are lost during the production of white flour, when the starchy part of the flour is separated from the bran and the germ. Wholewheat flour still contains the flour bran and germ, which are very rich in nutrients. The problem is, wholewheat muffins are often too compact. I prefer to use type 65 flour, a French white flour that is richer in nutrients than white flour but makes nice light muffins. However, this may be hard to find, so it's up to you to choose what you prefer.

A good muffin is…

A well-risen, dome-shaped cake, cracked and golden, well-coloured but not burnt on the edges and the bottom and with a moist, light sponge with plenty of fruit or other fillings.

1. Stay alert

Preparing the muffin mixture seems really simple but it's easy to mess up the measurements or to forget something. Stay calm and have fun, and don't get distracted. Even if you're an experimental cook, check that you haven't missed something before mixing the ingredients or, even more importantly, before cooking. And once the muffins are in the oven, try not to forget them. If you can smell burning, it's usually too late.

2. Don't mix too much

Don't mix the ingredients for too long – a few stirs with the whisk will do. There will still be lumps and bits of dry, unmixed flour here and there. Don't worry. It'll all mix together properly in the oven. If you mix too much you'll get too much gluten and will lose too much air, producing dry, compact muffins. This will also happen if you leave the mixture for too long before cooking. The raising agents, activated by the liquid, will become less and less active as time passes. Of course if you put the mixture in the fridge this will happen more slowly, but it's best to cook the muffins as soon as the mixture is ready.

Note: You can freeze the mixture in a container, defrost it and cook as usual or even freeze it in the muffin tray and cook straight from the freezer. For the latter, you will have to cook for longer.

3. Cooking

If you want well-risen muffins, soft in the middle and firm on the outside, your oven must be at the right temperature before cooking. I know that when we're busy, we can forget about instructions like "pre-heat the oven", but if you do not pre-heat the oven and you then increase the cooking time, your muffins will be dry. If, despite everything, you find that your muffins don't rise enough or that they are dry, you must increase the temperature. On the other hand if they are golden and well risen but aren't cooked on the inside, try again with a lower temperature.

Since every mixture and every oven is different, you will learn by trial and error. The usual cooking time is between 20 and 25 minutes. To check if a muffin is cooked through, stick a skewer in the centre. If it comes out dry, it is ready; if there is some mixture still stuck to it, return to the oven for a few minutes. One more thing: use eggs at room temperature.

100% chocolate

I'm not going to lie to you, this recipe isn't mine. It is largely inspired by the succulent chocolate cake my French mother-in-law makes. I've made a few small modifications and added some drops of coffee... and why not? Thank you Arlette!

Preparation time: 10 minutes
Cooking time: 10–15 minutes
Makes 12 muffins

Dry ingredients
80 g (2¾ oz) plain flour
1½ teaspoons baking powder
½ teaspoon salt

Wet ingredients
185 g (6½ oz) butter, melted and
  cooled
30 ml (1 fl oz) espresso coffee,
  cooled
185 g (6½ oz) caster sugar
5 eggs, separated
150 g (5¼ oz) dark chocolate,
  melted and cooled

Preheat the oven to 220°C (fan oven 200°C), Gas Mark 7.

Mix together the flour, baking powder and salt.

Mix together the butter, coffee and sugar to get a creamy paste, then add the egg yolks. Mix into the dry ingredients. Add the melted chocolate.

Beat the egg whites then fold into the mixture. Do not mix too much.

Pour the mixture into muffin moulds. Cook for 10–15 minutes until the muffins are well risen but still soft to the touch. These muffins must be really moist so don't overcook them, and don't forget that they will solidify somewhat when cooling.

Extra-moist blueberry muffins

When you hear the word muffin, what do you think of? A blueberry muffin! You find them all over the United States – and unfortunately they're not always the best. They're often too sweet, too dry, too big, with too few blueberries. Here is my version – an attempt to rectify this national dishonour...

Preparation time: 10 minutes
Cooking time: 10–20 minutes
Makes 12 muffins

Crumble
4 teaspoons butter, softened
2 dessertspoons plain flour
4 dessertspoons brown sugar
½ teaspoon cinnamon

Dry ingredients
320 g (11¼ oz) plain flour
3 teaspoons baking powder
150 g (5¼ oz) caster sugar

Wet ingredients
265 ml (9¼ fl oz) crème fraîche
65 ml (2¼ fl oz) sunflower oil
3 eggs
1 teaspoon vanilla extract
250 g (8¾ oz) blueberries

Preheat the oven to 220°C (fan oven 200°C), Gas Mark 7.

Prepare the crumble, mixing the ingredients together by hand or with a fork.

Mix all the dry ingredients together. Mix the wet ingredients together, except for the blueberries.

Combine the two mixtures without stirring too much.

Half-fill the muffin moulds with the combined mixture.

Share the blueberries between the moulds. Sink them into the mixture with a spoon or your finger. Fill the moulds to the top with the crumble.

Cook the muffins for 15–20 minutes until they are golden. Check they are cooked with a skewer; if it comes out clean, they are cooked.

Lemon and poppy seed muffins

In this recipe, the classic mix of lemon and poppy seed is deliciously complemented by small pieces of sweet juicy pear, which make the muffins really moist.

Preparation time: 15 minutes
Cooking time: 20–25 minutes
Makes 12 muffins

200 g (7 oz) peeled and cored pears (approx. 250 g/8¾ oz whole pears)

Icing
60 g (2 oz) icing sugar
2 dessertspoons lemon juice

Dry ingredients
320 g (11¼ oz) plain flour
3 dessertspoons poppy seeds
3 teaspoons baking powder
1 teaspoon salt
zest of 1½ lemons

Wet ingredients
125 g (4½ oz) butter, softened
150 g (5¼ oz) caster sugar
2 eggs, separated
210 ml (7½ fl oz) Greek yogurt
40 ml (1½ fl oz) lemon juice

Preheat the oven to 190°C (fan oven 170°C), Gas Mark 5.

Prepare the icing by mixing the icing sugar with the lemon juice.

Cut the pears into almond-sized pieces; if the pieces are too big, the mixture may sink during cooking.

Mix together the flour, poppy seeds, baking powder, salt and the zest of 1 lemon.

Beat the butter and sugar together for several minutes until you have a creamy, airy consistency. Whisk the egg whites until stiff.

Mix the yogurt and lemon juice together, making sure they come to 250 ml (8¾ fl oz) in total. Add the egg yolks to the butter and sugar, then the yogurt and lemon juice, then the egg whites.

Little by little, mix in the dry ingredients and the pear pieces without over working the mixture.

Divide the mixture between the muffin moulds and garnish with the rest of the lemon zest.

Cook the muffins for 20–25 minutes until they are firm and golden. Check they are cooked through with a skewer; if it comes out clean, they are done. When they have cooled down, ice the muffins using a spoon.

Tip: 1½ lemons should provide enough juice for both the icing and the muffin mix.

Chocolate chip muffins

Even though this is a classic recipe, chocolate chip muffins give muffins in general a bad image. Unlike typical chocolate chip muffins, this recipe is light and moist and full of chocolate chips. Choose a good quality chocolate as you will taste the difference.

Preparation time: 10 minutes
Cooking time: 20–25 minutes
Makes 12 muffins

Dry ingredients
320 g (11¼ oz) plain flour
50 g (1¾ oz) caster sugar
3 teaspoons baking powder
1 teaspoon salt
150 g (5¼ oz) chocolate, broken into
  small irregular chips

Wet ingredients
1 egg, separated
325 ml (11½ fl oz) crème fraîche
175 ml (6¼ fl oz) semi-skimmed
  milk
50 ml (1¾ fl oz) sunflower oil
1 teaspoon vanilla extract

Preheat the oven to 200°C (fan oven 180°C), Gas Mark 6.

Mix the flour, sugar, baking powder and salt together. Add the egg yolk.

Whisk the egg white until stiff.

Mix the remaining wet ingredients with the dry ingredients then add the egg white and chocolate chips. There is no need to mix the ingredients together too much.

Divide the mixture between the muffin moulds. Cook the muffins for 20–25 minutes until they are firm and golden. Check they are cooked through with a skewer; if it comes out clean, they are done.

Rhubarb and strawberry muffins

I find it odd to think that, at some point in history, someone discovered how good it was to eat rhubarb and strawberries together. Imagine that for years before this discovery people had lived without ever tasting this wonderful combination. Not easy! Here is my meagre contribution to this glorious tradition of cooking with rhubarb and strawberries.

Preparation time: 10 minutes
Cooking time: 15–20 minutes
Makes 12 muffins

75 g (2½ oz) rhubarb, cut into pieces
175 g (6¼ oz) strawberries, cut into pieces

Crumble topping
4 teaspoons butter, softened
2 dessertspoons plain flour
4 dessertspoons brown sugar
½ teaspoon cinnamon

Dry ingredients
320 g (11¼ oz) plain flour
3 teaspoons baking powder
150 g (5¼ oz) caster sugar

Wet ingredients
265 ml (9¼ fl oz) crème fraîche
65 ml (2¼ fl oz) sunflower oil
3 eggs
1 teaspoon vanilla extract

Preheat the oven to 220°C (fan oven 200°C), Gas Mark 7.

Prepare the crumble topping by mixing the ingredients together by hand or with a fork.

Mix the dry ingredients together. Add the rhubarb and strawberry pieces.

Mix the wet ingredients together.

Combine the dry and wet ingredients together, without stirring too much.

Fill the muffin moulds three-quarters full and finish with the crumble topping.

Cook the muffins for 15–20 minutes until they are firm and golden. Check they are cooked through with a skewer; if it comes out clean, they are done.

Raspberry muffins

Nothing could be easier than this recipe! The butter-based batter is a bit like biscuit mix – it's fairly plain to allow the anti-oxidant rich raspberries to shine through.

Preparation time: 10 minutes
Cooking time: 20–25 minutes
Makes 12 muffins

400 g (14 oz) plain flour
4 teaspoons baking powder
75 g (2½ oz) caster sugar
1 teaspoon salt
175 g (6¼ oz) butter, softened
250 ml (8¾ fl oz) semi-skimmed
  milk
350 g (12¼ oz) raspberries

Preheat the oven to 200°C (fan oven 180°C), Gas Mark 6.

Mix together the flour, baking powder, sugar and salt.

Add the butter, mixing with your hands (or with a fork), then add the milk little by little.

Fill the muffin moulds to halfway. Add a few raspberries to each mould and push in with a spoon or finger. If the moulds are less than three-quarters full, you could add a few more raspberries.

Cook the muffins for 20–25 minutes until they are firm and golden. Check they are cooked through with a skewer; if it comes out clean, they are done.

Gingerbread muffins

Gingerbread is a traditional Christmas cake. Here is an adapted recipe, with big chunks of juicy Granny Smith apples, which will make you think it's Christmas all year!

Preparation time: 15 minutes
Cooking time: 20–25 minutes
Makes 12 muffins

325 g (11½ oz) peeled and cored
  Granny Smith apples (approx.
  375 g/13¼ oz whole apples)
juice of 1 lemon

Dry ingredients
240 g (8½ oz) plain flour
75 g (2½ oz) rolled oats
3 teaspoons baking powder
50 g (1¾ oz) raisins
3 teaspoons ground ginger
5 teaspoons cinnamon
1 teaspoon salt
zest of 1 lemon
110 g (4 oz) brown sugar

Wet ingredients
150 ml (5¼ fl oz) semi-skimmed
  milk
110 ml (4 fl oz) sunflower oil
2 eggs

Preheat the oven to 205°C (fan oven 185°C), Gas Mark 6.

Mix all the dry ingredients together, keeping aside a little of the lemon zest and brown sugar to decorate the tops of the muffins.

Crush two-thirds of the apples and cut the rest into almond-sized pieces. Squeeze the lemon juice over all the prepared apples. Add the apples to the dry ingredients and mix until covered by flour.

Mix the milk, oil and eggs together. Combine the wet and dry ingredients without stirring too much.

Divide the mixture between the muffin moulds and garnish with the remaining lemon zest and brown sugar.

Cook the muffins for 20–25 minutes until they are firm and golden. Check they are cooked through with a skewer; if it comes out clean, they are done.

Chocolate orange muffins

I created this recipe for my wife. She pestered me for years to make muffins like a particular marble cake she loved when we lived in Los Angeles. After several attempts and a few mistakes I found one she liked... she just has to find a new reason to annoy me now!

Preparation time: 10 minutes
Cooking time: 15–20 minutes
Makes 12 muffins

Chocolate mixture
90 g (3 oz) butter, softened
90 g (3 oz) caster sugar
2 eggs, separated
40 g (1½ oz) plain flour
75 g (2½ oz) dark chocolate, melted
  and cooled

Orange mixture
190 g (6¾ oz) plain flour
1½ teaspoons baking powder
170 g (6 oz) butter, softened
150 g (5¼ oz) caster sugar
1 teaspoon vanilla extract
3 eggs, separated
zest of 2 oranges

Preheat the oven to 210°C (fan oven 190°C), Gas Mark 6.

Prepare the chocolate mixture. Beat the butter and sugar together for several minutes to get a smooth, light cream. Whisk the egg whites to stiff peaks. Mix the butter and sugar with the egg yolks, flour, melted chocolate and finally the egg whites. Mix until the flour is incorporated but no more.

Prepare the orange mixture. Mix the flour and baking powder together. Vigorously beat the butter with the sugar and vanilla extract until you have a smooth, light cream. Whisk the egg whites until stiff. Mix the butter and sugar with the egg yolks, flour, orange zest and finally the egg whites. Mix until the flour is incorporated but no more.

Half-fill the moulds with the orange mixture. With a spoon or your finger, make a well in the mixture and fill it with the chocolate mixture.

Cook the muffins for 15–20 minutes until they are firm and golden. Check they are cooked through with a skewer; if it comes out clean, they are done.

Carrot cake muffins

In this dairy-free carrot cake, apples, oranges and beetroot make the batter moist and provide a delicate flavour. And, in case you didn't know, carrots are rich in beta-carotene, which is good for the skin and sight.

Preparation time: 20 minutes
Cooking time: 20–25 minutes
Makes 12 muffins

Dry ingredients
255 g (9 oz) plain flour
80 g (2¾ oz) rolled oats
3 teaspoons baking powder
140 g (5 oz) brown sugar
40 g (1½ oz) nuts, finely chopped
40 g (1½ oz) raisins
zest of 1 orange
4 teaspoons cinnamon
1 teaspoon grated nutmeg
1 teaspoon salt

Wet ingredients
5 eggs
120 ml (4¼ fl oz) sunflower oil
juice of 1 orange
200 g (7 oz) peeled, cored and
    grated apples (approx. 230 g/8 oz
    whole apples)
150 g (5¼ oz) grated carrots
    (approx. 165 g/5¾ oz whole
    carrots)
50 g (1¾ oz) peeled and grated raw
    beetroot

Preheat the oven to 200°C (fan oven 180°C), Gas Mark 6.

Mix the flour, oats and baking powder together, keeping a few oats to decorate the muffins. Add the other dry ingredients.

Mix the eggs and oil together. Add the other wet ingredients.

Mix the two sets of ingredients together without stirring too much.

Divide the mixture between the muffin moulds. You can fill them to the top as they won't rise a lot during cooking. Sprinkle with the remaining oats.

Cook the muffins for 20–25 minutes until they are firm and golden. Check they are cooked through with a skewer; if it comes out clean, they are done.

Tip: If you can't find raw beetroot, you could replace it with cooked beetroot or, if you prefer a more traditional carrot cake, replace it with extra grated carrot.

Pumpkin muffins

I'm sure you love pumpkins. They are funny and full of beta-carotene, vitamin C and fibre. I love to cut open a pumpkin and remove the seeds. It's my hunting streak coming to the surface. And to celebrate this prize... a moist, light pumpkin muffin, filled with a little surprise mouthful of fromage frais!

Preparation time: 15 minutes
Cooking time: 15–20 minutes
Makes 12 muffins

400 g (14 oz) raw pumpkin flesh, crushed
100 g (3½ oz) fromage frais

Dry ingredients
340 g (12 oz) plain flour
3 teaspoons baking powder
150 g (5¼ oz) brown sugar
1 dessertspoon cinnamon
1 teaspoon ground ginger
1 teaspoon salt
½ teaspoon grated nutmeg

Wet ingredients
80 ml (2¾ fl oz) buttermilk
120 ml (4¼ fl oz) sunflower oil
2 eggs
1 teaspoon vanilla extract

Preheat the oven to 210°C (fan oven 190°C), Gas Mark 6.

Mix all the dry ingredients together.

Mix the buttermilk, oil, eggs and vanilla extract together.

Combine the wet and dry ingredients, add the pumpkin and mix without overworking the batter.

Fill the muffin moulds to halfway, put a good teaspoon of fromage frais in the centre of each and fill the moulds to the top with the rest of the muffin mixture.

Cook the muffins for 15–20 minutes until they are firm and golden. Check they are cooked through with a skewer; if it comes out clean, they are done (unless you hit the fromage frais, which will stay soft).

Tip: Don't forget to peel the pumpkin. If you have difficulty getting to the raw flesh, cut the pumpkin in half and cook in the oven, flesh side down, for 45 minutes at 180°C (fan oven 160°C), Gas Mark 4. You should then be able to scoop out the flesh easily with a spoon.

Sour cherry muffins

I love sour cherries. When I was little, I ate cherry pies from McDonald's all the time. Today, I treat myself with these muffins. In this recipe, the apple makes the muffins moist and gives them an additional sweetness.

Preparation time: 20 minutes
Cooking time: 20–25 minutes
Makes 12 muffins

185 g (6½ oz) peeled, cored and grated apples (approx. 230 g/ 8 oz whole apples)
185 g (6½ oz) morello cherries, stoned and cut into quarters

Dry ingredients
240 g (8½ oz) plain flour
75 g (2½ oz) rolled oats
3 teaspoons baking powder
1 dessertspoon cinnamon
1 teaspoon salt
110 g (4 oz) caster sugar

Wet ingredients
150 ml (5¼ fl oz) semi-skimmed milk
110 ml (4 fl oz) sunflower oil
2 eggs

Preheat the oven to 205°C (fan oven 185°C), Gas Mark 6.

Mix all the dry ingredients together, saving a little sugar to decorate the top of the muffins.

Add the apples and cherries and mix until they are covered with flour.

Mix the wet ingredients together, then combine the wet and dry ingredients without overworking the batter.

Divide the muffin mix between the moulds and sprinkle with the remaining sugar.

Cook the muffins for 20–25 minutes until they are firm and golden. Check they are cooked through with a skewer; if it comes out clean, they are done.

Tip: Make sure you cut the cherries into quarters before using; if the cherries are too large, they'll make the muffins overflow during cooking.

Pear muffins

One day I found myself with several kilos of very ripe pears. I thought it was stupid to throw them away, so I decided to make muffins with them... that's how I invented this recipe, which is now a firm favourite.

Preparation time: 20 minutes
Cooking time: 20–25 minutes
Makes 12 muffins

225 g (8 oz) peeled, cored and grated apples (approx. 300 g /10½ oz whole apples)
150 g (5¼ oz) peeled and cored pears, cut into pieces (approx. 200 g/7 oz whole pears)

Dry ingredients
240 g (8½ oz) plain flour
75 g (2½ oz) rolled oats
3 teaspoons baking powder
1 dessertspoon cinnamon
1 teaspoon salt
85 g (3 oz) caster sugar

Wet ingredients
150 ml (5¼ fl oz) semi-skimmed milk
110 ml (4 fl oz) sunflower oil
2 eggs

Preheat the oven to 205°C (fan oven 185°C), Gas Mark 6.

Mix all the dry ingredients together, keeping aside a little sugar to decorate the muffins.

Add the apples and pears and mix until they are covered with flour.

Mix the wet ingredients together and add to the dry mixture without stirring too much.

Divide the mixture between the muffin moulds and sprinkle with the remaining sugar.

Cook the muffins for 20–25 minutes until they are firm and golden. Check they are cooked through with a skewer; if it comes out clean, they are done.

Matcha (green tea) muffins

The key ingredient of this recipe is Matcha, a finely ground Japanese green tea. These green muffins seem to come straight from Mars, but I promise you there's nothing to be afraid of, except for never finding out what they taste like…

Preparation time: 10 minutes
Cooking time: 20–25 minutes
Makes 12 muffins

255 g (9 oz) plain flour
20 g (¾ oz) Matcha tea
2 teaspoons baking powder
330 g (11½ oz) butter, softened
300 g (10½ oz) caster sugar
7 eggs, separated
100 g (3½ oz) white chocolate,
  broken into small, irregular pieces
50 g (1¾ oz) pine nuts

Preheat the oven to 200°C (fan oven 180°C), Gas Mark 6.

Mix the flour, tea and baking powder together.

Beat the butter and sugar together for several minutes until you have a smooth, light cream.

Whisk the egg whites until stiff.

Add the egg yolks to the butter and sugar then mix into the flour mixture. Finally mix in the egg whites. Try not to overwork the mixture.

Divide the batter between the muffin moulds. You can fill them to the top as this mixture is quite dense.

Sprinkle the chocolate pieces evenly over the muffins and sink them into the surfaces. After cooking you will no longer be able to see the chocolate but you will still be able to taste it.

Garnish the muffins with the pine nuts and press lightly into the surfaces. Place them near the centre of each muffin or they may fall off during cooking.

Cook the muffins for 20–25 minutes until they are firm and golden. Check they are cooked through with a skewer; if it comes out clean, they are done.

Mango time muffins

These sweet and spicy muffins have a base of fresh mango and mango chutney. Before starting the recipe, check your mango is really ripe. They should give lightly when you press them and smell quite fruity. These muffins are excellent warm. Serve alone or accompanied by a spicy meal.

Preparation time: 15 minutes
Cooking time: 20–25 minutes
Makes 12 muffins

400 g (14 oz) plain flour
4 teaspoons baking powder
50 g (1¾ oz) caster sugar
1 teaspoon salt
175 g (6¼ oz) butter, softened
250 ml (8¾ fl oz) semi-skimmed milk
250 g (8¾ oz) fresh mango, peeled and cut into pieces
100 g (3½ oz) mango chutney

Preheat the oven to 200°C (fan oven 180°C), Gas Mark 6.

Mix the flour, baking powder, sugar and salt together.

Mix in the butter by hand or with a fork, then add the milk, little by little.

Mix the fresh mango with the chutney. Mix into the batter.

Divide the mixture between the muffin moulds.

Cook the muffins for 20–25 minutes until they are firm and golden. Check they are cooked through with a skewer; if it comes out clean, they are done.

Dulce de leche muffins by La Cocotte

The recipe for these succulent, marbled, cheesecake muffins comes from La Cocotte, a specialist food bookshop in the 11th arrondissement of Paris. As well as offering the most amazing collection of cookery books and utensils, the shop has elevated dulce de leche to an art form.

Preparation time: 15 minutes
Cooking time: 30–35 minutes
Makes 12 muffins

50 g (1¾ oz) dulce de leche
50 g (1¾ oz) walnuts, chopped

Muffin mixture
270 g (9½ oz) plain flour
2 teaspoons baking powder
50 g (1¾ oz) caster sugar
2 eggs
100 ml (3½ fl oz) milk
80 ml (2¾ fl oz) vegetable oil
250 g (8¾ oz) dulce de leche
125 g (4½ oz) walnuts, chopped

Cheesecake mixture
125 g (4½ oz) ricotta
75 g (2½ oz) fromage frais
2 dessertspoons crème fraîche
2 dessertspoons caster sugar
1 egg
1 teaspoon vanilla extract
3 dessertspoons plain flour

Preheat the oven to 180°C (fan oven 160°C), Gas Mark 4.

Prepare the muffin mixture. Sieve the flour and baking powder together. Mix the sugar, eggs, milk, oil and dulce de leche into a runny paste. Mix in the flour and then the walnuts.

Prepare the cheesecake mix by mixing all the ingredients together until there are no lumps.

Put one dessertspoon of muffin mixture into each mould, add a rounded teaspoon of dulce de leche then one dessertspoon of cheesecake mix. Lightly mix with a skewer or knife. Sprinkle with the chopped nuts.

Cook for 30–35 minutes.

Courgette muffins

If you've only ever eaten courgettes in savoury dishes, prepare yourself for a nice surprise. In these dairy-free muffins, the small, slightly sour pieces of Granny Smith apples marry beautifully with the green and white batons of soft, delicately flavoured courgettes.

Preparation time: 20 minutes
Cooking time: 20–25 minutes
Makes 12 muffins

12 thin strips of courgette peel

Dry ingredients
320 g (11¼ oz) plain flour
3 teaspoons baking powder
50 g (1¾ oz) walnuts, finely
  chopped
50 g (1¾ oz) raisins
2 teaspoons cinnamon
1 teaspoon salt
150 g (5¼ oz) caster sugar

Wet ingredients
4 eggs
150 ml (5¼ fl oz) sunflower oil
150 g (5¼ oz) peeled, cored and
  grated Granny Smith apples
  (approx. 175 g/6¼ oz whole
  apples)
150 g (5¼ oz) grated courgettes
  (approx. 165 g /5¾ oz whole
  courgettes)

Preheat the oven to 200°C (fan oven 180°C), Gas Mark 6.

Sieve the flour and baking powder together then mix with the other dry ingredients, saving a little of the sugar to sprinkle on top of the muffins.

Mix the eggs and oil together. Add the apples and courgettes.

Mix the dry and wet ingredients together without overworking them.

Divide the mixture between the muffin moulds. Decorate each with a strip of courgette peel and a pinch of sugar.

Cook the muffins for 20–25 minutes until they are firm and golden. Check they are cooked through with a skewer; if it comes out clean, they are done.

Banana muffins

From time to time, friends tell me they don't like bananas. For me, that's like saying they don't like the sun. Even if you are one of these "bananaphobics", you must try this extra-moist recipe, inspired by banana bread, with coconut milk, dates and pecan nuts.

Preparation time: 20 minutes
Cooking time: 20–25 minutes
Makes 12 muffins

75 g (2½ oz) dried dates

Dry ingredients
240 g (8½ oz) plain flour
75 g (2½ oz) rolled oats
3 teaspoons baking powder
40 g (1½ oz) pecan nuts, chopped
2 dessertspoons cinnamon
1 teaspoon salt
55 g (2 oz) brown sugar

Wet ingredients
190 g (6¾ oz) Greek yogurt
115 ml (4 oz) sunflower oil
75 ml (2½ oz) coconut milk
60 g (2 oz) honey, preferably acacia
3 eggs
1 teaspoon vanilla extract
225 g (8 oz) peeled bananas,
  mashed

Preheat the oven to 180°C (fan oven 160°C), Gas Mark 4.

Soak the dates in boiling water for around 10 minutes.

Mix all the dry ingredients together, setting aside a little brown sugar to decorate the muffins.

Mix all the wet ingredients together except the bananas.

Drain the dates, remove the stones and chop finely. Mix the bananas and dates with the wet ingredients.

Mix the wet and dry ingredients together without overworking the mixture.

Divide the mixture between the muffin moulds. You can fill them to the top.

Cook the muffins for 20–25 minutes until they are firm and golden. Check they are cooked through with a skewer; if it comes out clean, they are done.

Tip: For the dates, 75 g (2½ oz) is the weight with their stones. Rehydrated and stoned dates will weigh around the same.

Orange, sweet potato and bilberry muffins

If you're in need of some sunshine, taste these sweet, colourful muffins and you'll feel better right away! Without fat or dairy products, full of beta-carotene and vitamin C, and absolutely delicious, these muffins have everything.

Preparation time: 40 minutes
Cooking time: 15–20 minutes
Makes 12 muffins

150 g (5¼ oz) dried bilberries

Dry ingredients
320 g (11¼ oz) plain flour
3 teaspoons baking powder
40 g (1½ oz) brown sugar
1 dessertspoon cinnamon
1 teaspoon salt
½ teaspoon grated nutmeg
zest of 2 oranges
50 g (1¾ oz) pecans, finely chopped

Wet ingredients
300 ml (10½ fl oz) freshly squeezed
  orange juice
4 eggs
250 g (8¾ oz) sweet potatoes,
  cooked, peeled, cooled and
  mashed

Preheat the oven to 200°C (fan oven 180°C), Gas Mark 6.

Soak the bilberries in boiling water for 5 minutes.

Mix all the dry ingredients together.

Mix all the wet ingredients together.

Combine the wet and dry ingredients together. Drain and add the bilberries. Make sure you don't stir the mixture more than necessary.

Divide the mixture between the muffin moulds.

Cook the muffins for 15–20 minutes until they are firm and golden. Check they are cooked through with a skewer; if it comes out clean, they are done.

Quaker-style muffins

As well as having a pleasant texture and a delicious taste, durum wheat is an excellent source of fibre. Here it is in a moist, fruity adaptation of a classic American muffin, with a French touch – goat's cheese and figs!

Preparation time: 20 minutes
Cooking time: 20–25 minutes
Makes 12 muffins

250 g (8¾ oz) peeled, cored and grated apples (approx. 280 g/10 oz whole apples)
250 g (8¾ oz) fresh figs cut into pieces (approx. 275 g/9¾ oz whole figs)
100 g (3½ oz) soft goat's cheese

Dry ingredients
240 g (8½ oz) plain flour
100 g (3½ oz) durum wheat
175 g (6¼ oz) brown sugar
3 teaspoons baking powder
1 teaspoon salt

Wet ingredients
185 ml (6½ fl oz) milk
185 ml (6½ fl oz) sunflower oil
3 eggs

Preheat the oven to 190°C (fan oven 170°C), Gas Mark 5.

Mix the dry ingredients together. Add the grated apples and fig pieces. Mix the wet ingredients together and add to the dry mixture.

Fill the muffin moulds halfway full, add a round teaspoon of goat's cheese to each and cover with the rest of the mixture. You can fill to the top of the moulds.

Cook the muffins for 20–25 minutes until they are firm and golden. Check they are cooked through with a skewer; if it comes out dry, they are done (unless you pierce the cheese, which will be soft).

Coffee cake muffins

Without wanting to show off, my special "Pause Café" muffins are the best. The crumble topping is even but not too smooth and the sponge is moist and naturally sweet thanks to the apple. And, unlike some coffee cakes, my muffins actually contain coffee!

Preparation time: 10 minutes
Cooking time: 20–25 minutes
Makes 12 muffins

Espresso filling
2 dessertspoons ground coffee
4 dessertspoons ground almonds
4 dessertspoons brown sugar

Crumble topping
4 teaspoons butter, softened
2 dessertspoons plain flour
4 dessertspoons brown sugar

Dry ingredients
240 g (8½ oz) plain flour
75 g (2½ oz) rolled oats
3 teaspoons baking powder
85 g (3 oz) caster sugar
1 dessertspoon cinnamon
1 teaspoon salt

Wet ingredients
150 ml (5¼ fl oz) milk
110 ml (4 fl oz) sunflower oil
2 eggs
260 g (9 oz) peeled, cored and
  grated apples (approx. 325 g/ 11 ½
  oz whole apples)

Preheat the oven to 205°C (fan oven 185°C), Gas Mark 6.

Prepare the espresso filling by mixing together all the ingredients.

Prepare the crumble topping by mixing all the ingredients together by hand or with a fork. Mix in 1 dessertspoon of the espresso filling.

Mix all the dry ingredients together. Mix all the wet ingredients together except the apples. Mix the dry and wet ingredients together and add the apples without overworking.

Fill the muffin moulds halfway. Add two teaspoons of espresso filling to each muffin and stir once or twice to mix with the batter. Be careful not to mix it in entirely.

Add a little more batter then fill the moulds to the top with the crumble topping.

Cook the muffins for 20–25 minutes until they are firm and golden. Check they are cooked through with a skewer; if it comes out clean, they are done.

Caramel muffins

You have been warned – these muffins are dangerously good. So good that I don't like to make them too often as I eat too many. A bit of advice: eat in moderation! Two or three muffins – all will be fine. Four or five – too many, but still OK. By the seventh – perhaps it's time to get help… or at least to wash your hands.

Preparation time: 25 minutes
Cooking time: 20–25 minutes
Makes 12 muffins

185 g (6½ oz) dried dates
115 g (4 oz) peeled, cored and grated apples (approx. 175 g/ 6¼ oz whole apples)
150 ml (5¼ fl oz) dulce de leche

Dry ingredients
240 g (8½ oz) plain flour
75 g (2½ oz) rolled oats
3 teaspoons baking powder
40 g (1½ oz) brown sugar
1 teaspoon salt

Wet ingredients
150 ml (5¼ fl oz) semi-skimmed milk
110 ml (4 fl oz) sunflower oil
2 eggs

Preheat the oven to 205°C (fan oven 185°C), Gas Mark 6.

Soak the dates in boiling water for around 10 minutes.

Mix all the dry ingredients together then add the grated apples. Mix the wet ingredients together.

Drain the dates, stone them and chop or mash them to get a sticky paste.

Mix the wet and dry ingredients together without overworking the mixture.

Fill the muffin moulds halfway full. Add a spoonful of date paste and a spoonful of dulce de leche to each muffin. Add more muffin mixture then add a small bit of date paste and dulce de leche for decoration (the majority should be inside).

Cook the muffins for 20–25 minutes until they are firm and golden. Check they are cooked through with a skewer; if it comes out clean, they are done. If the tops of the muffins start burning before they are cooked through, cover them with aluminium foil. I would also recommend putting aluminium foil under your moulds so they don't get your oven dirty. It is difficult to keep clean when making these muffins!

Tip: 185 g (6½ oz) is the weight of the dates with their stones. Rehydrated and stoned dates will weigh around the same.

Chocolate and coconut muffins

The addition of coconut gives these muffins a slightly tropical taste. Even though the fatty acids in the coconut are saturated, the muffins are mostly healthy.

Preparation time: 10 minutes
Cooking time: 20–25 minutes
Makes 12 muffins

Dry ingredients
105 g (3¾ oz) plain flour
300 g (10½ oz) caster sugar
1 teaspoon baking powder
85 g (3 oz) unsweetened
  cocoa powder
50 g (1¾ oz) desiccated coconut

Wet ingredients
165 ml (5¾ fl oz) sunflower oil
65 ml (2¼ fl oz) coconut milk
4 eggs, separated

Preheat the oven to 200°C (fan oven 180°C), Gas Mark 6.

Mix all the dry ingredients together, keeping a little coconut aside to decorate the muffins.

Mix the oil, coconut milk and the egg yolks together.

Whisk the egg whites until stiff.

Mix the wet and dry ingredients together then add the egg whites, mixing gently without overworking the batter.

Divide the batter between the muffin moulds then garnish with the remaining coconut.

Cook the muffins for 20–25 minutes until they are firm and golden. Check they are cooked through with a skewer; if it comes out clean, they are done.

Strawberry and ricotta muffins

Lots of strawberries and a moist, oozing centre. Not too sweet, a bit like a cheesecake. What more can I say?

Preparation time: 15 minutes
Cooking time: 15–20 minutes
Makes 12 muffins

Dry ingredients
400 g (14 oz) plain flour
4 teaspoons baking powder
150 g (5¼ oz) caster sugar
1 teaspoon salt

Wet ingredients
300 g (10½ oz) ricotta
85 ml (3 fl oz) sunflower oil
85 ml (3 fl oz) semi-skimmed milk
2 eggs, separated
300 g (10½ oz) strawberries, cut
 into small pieces

Preheat the oven to 185°C (fan oven 165°C), Gas Mark 4.

Mix all the dry ingredients together.

Mix the ricotta, oil, milk and egg yolks together.

Whisk the egg whites until stiff.

Mix everything together, including the egg whites and strawberries, without overworking the mixture.

Cook the muffins for 15–20 minutes until they are firm and golden. Check they are cooked through with a skewer; if it comes out clean, they are done.

Almond cherry muffins

Almonds are the perfect example of a healthy food that is also delicious. They are an excellent source of protein, healthy fats, magnesium, potassium and vitamin E. In this recipe, ground almonds and almond paste delicately complement juicy cherries for an irresistible result.

Preparation time: 15 minutes
Cooking time: 20–25 minutes
Makes 12 muffins

Crumble topping
2 teaspoons butter, softened
2 teaspoons almond paste
2 dessertspoons plain flour
4 dessertspoons brown sugar

Dry ingredients
320 g (11¼ oz) plain flour
3 teaspoons baking powder
150 g (5¼ oz) caster sugar
125 g (4½ oz) ground almonds
1 teaspoon salt

Wet ingredients
250 ml (8¾ fl oz) buttermilk
125 ml (4½ fl oz) sunflower oil
2 eggs
150 g (5¼ oz) cherries, stoned
   and quartered

Preheat the oven to 200°C (fan oven 180°C), Gas Mark 6.

Prepare the crumble topping. Mix the butter and almond paste together by hand or with a fork. Add the flour then the brown sugar.

Mix all the dry ingredients together. Mix all the wet ingredients together. Mix the wet and dry ingredients together without overworking the batter.

Fill the muffin moulds two-thirds full with the mixture then top with the crumble topping. You can fill to the top of the moulds.

Cook the muffins for 20–25 minutes until they are firm and golden. Check they are cooked through with a skewer; if it comes out clean, they are done.

Tip: Make sure you cut the cherries into small pieces. If the pieces are too big, the muffins may overflow during cooking.

Blueberry and maize flour muffins

These muffins are less sweet than traditional blueberry muffins and look less like cake. Made with buttermilk, they taste a bit like cornbread, so are excellent for breakfast.

Preparation time: 10 minutes
Cooking time: 15–20 minutes
Makes 12 muffins

180 g (6¼ oz) blueberries

Dry ingredients
190 g (6¾ oz) plain flour
210 g (7½ oz) maize flour
3 teaspoons baking powder
1 teaspoon salt
75 g (2½ oz) caster sugar

Wet ingredients
400 ml (14 fl oz) buttermilk
75 g (2½ oz) butter, melted
2 eggs

Preheat the oven to 220°C (fan oven 200°C), Gas Mark 7.

Mix all the dry ingredients together, keeping a little of the sugar aside to decorate the tops of the muffins.

Add the blueberries.

Mix the wet ingredients together.

Mix the wet and dry ingredients together without overmixing the batter. It should become quite purple.

Divide the mixture between the muffin moulds and sprinkle them with the remaining sugar.

Cook the muffins for 15–20 minutes until they are firm and golden. Check they are cooked through with a skewer; if it comes out clean, they are done.

Kugel (noodle pudding muffins)

When I was little, one of the reasons I loved visiting my grandmother in Brooklyn was Kugel. It is delicious served hot with a spicy meal or cold for dessert. I have always liked to eat them fresh from the fridge with some cold chicken for a midnight feast.

Preparation time: 20 minutes
Cooking time: 30–35 minutes
Makes 12 muffins

175 g (6¼ oz) dried egg noodles
100 g (3½ oz) dried bilberries or
  raisins
45 g (1½ oz) plain flour
½ teaspoon baking powder
1 teaspoon salt
2 dessertspoons cinnamon
5 eggs
35 ml (1¼ fl oz) sunflower oil
175 g (6¼ oz) sugar-free apple
  compote
75 g (2½ oz) honey, preferably
  acacia
1 teaspoon vanilla extract
175 g (6¼ oz) peeled and cored
  Granny Smith apples, cut into
  small pieces (approx. 200 g/7 oz
  whole apples)

Preheat the oven to 185°C (fan oven 165°C), Gas Mark 4.

Cook the noodles until they are al dente then drain and rinse them in cold water. Drain again.

Soak the dried bilberries in boiling water for several minutes.

Mix the flour, baking powder, salt and cinnamon together.

Mix the eggs, oil, apple compote, honey and vanilla extract together, then combine with the flour mixture.

Add the cold noodles, drained bilberries and chopped apples.

Divide the mixture between the muffin moulds. You can fill them all the way as the muffins won't rise much. If you use raisins, sink them into the muffins as they will burn if they are too near the surface.

Cook the muffins for 30–35 minutes until they are golden and the batter no longer bubbles. If you think the muffins will burn before they are cooked through, cover them with some aluminium foil.

Cornbread muffins

Cornbread always makes me nostalgic – and not just becaue I'm American. No, I think it has something that takes you down memory lane. With a guacamole icing, these muffins are almost a meal in themselves.

Preparation time: 15 minutes + cooling
Cooking time: 15–20 minutes
Makes 12 muffins

Dry ingredients
190 g (6¾ oz) plain flour
210 g (7½ oz) maize flour
3 teaspoons baking powder
1 teaspoon salt

Wet ingredients
400 ml (14 fl oz) buttermilk
75 g (2½ oz) butter, melted
2 eggs
180 g (6¼ oz) sweetcorn
½ green chilli, deseeded and finely chopped

Guacamole icing
flesh from 1 ripe avocado
juice of ½ lime
½ chilli, deseeded and finely chopped
1 cherry tomato, finely chopped
1 dessertspoon ground coriander
1 teaspoon salt
½ teaspoon black pepper
1 teaspoon olive oil

Preheat the oven to 220°C (fan oven 200°C), Gas Mark 7.

Mix all the dry ingredients together.

Mix all the wet ingredients together with a hand-held mixer or in a blender to mix in the sweetcorn and chilli.

Mix the wet and dry ingredients together without overworking the batter.

Divide the mixture between the muffin moulds. Cook the muffins for 15–20 minutes until they are firm and golden. Check they are cooked through with a skewer; if it comes out clean, they are done.

Leave the muffins to cool.

Mix all the guacamole ingredients together and ice the cold muffins.

Gluten-free banana caramel muffins

In New York, gluten-free food is very fashionable, not only for health reasons but also because more and more people find it easier to digest. These muffins are especially good lightly grilled and served with butter, honey or jam.

Preparation time: 15 minutes
Cooking time: 15–20 minutes
Makes 12 muffins

150 g (5¼ oz) salted butter caramels, cut into small pieces

Dry ingredients
500 g (1 lb 1½ oz) rice flour
3 teaspoons gluten-free baking powder
60 g (2 oz) brown sugar
1 teaspoon cinnamon
1 teaspoon salt

Wet ingredients
250 ml (8¾ fl oz) milk
75 ml (2½ fl oz) sunflower oil
3 eggs
1 teaspoon vanilla extract
200 g (7 oz) peeled ripe bananas, mashed

Preheat the oven to 210°C (fan oven 190°C), Gas Mark 6.

Mix all the dry ingredients together.

Mix all the wet ingredients together.

Combine the wet and dry ingredients together without overworking the batter.

Divide the mixture between the muffin moulds. Divide the caramels between the moulds and sink into the batter with your finger or a spoon.

Cook the muffins for 15–20 minutes until they are firm and golden. Check they are cooked through with a skewer; if it comes out clean, they are done (unless you pierce the caramel, which will melt on cooking).

Tip: You can find rice flour and gluten-free baking powder in most health food stores and in large supermarkets.

Index

Acknowledgements

With thanks to the following:

Jean-Pierre Ahtuam
Steven Alan
Arlette Coron
Fabienne Coron
Gabriel Coron
Damien de Meideros
Vianney de Seze
Tore Dokkedahl
Jerry Grant
Roslyn Grant
Ingrid Janowski
Rachel Khoo
Benoît le Thierry d'Ennequin
Amaury Reboulh de Veyrac Blin de Grincourt
Jennifer Wagner
Andrea Wainer

Conversion tables

The tables below are only approximate and are meant to be used as a guide only.

Approximate American/ European conversions

	USA	Metric	Imperial
brown sugar	1 cup	170 g	6 oz
butter	1 stick	115 g	4 oz
butter/ margarine/ lard	1 cup	225 g	8 oz
caster and granulated sugar	2 level tablespoons	30 g	1 oz
caster and granulated sugar	1 cup	225 g	8 oz
currants	1 cup	140 g	5 oz
flour	1 cup	140 g	5 oz
golden syrup	1 cup	350 g	12 oz
ground almonds	1 cup	115 g	4 oz
sultanas/ raisins	1 cup	200 g	7 oz

Approximate American/ European conversions

American	European
1 teaspoon	1 teaspoon/ 5 ml
½ fl oz	1 tablespoon/ ½ fl oz/ 15 ml
¼ cup	4 tablespoons/ 2 fl oz/ 50 ml
½ cup plus 2 tablespoons	¼ pint/ 5 fl oz/ 150 ml
1¼ cups	½ pint/ 10 fl oz/ 300 ml
1 pint/ 16 fl oz	1 pint/ 20 fl oz/ 600 ml
2½ pints (5 cups)	1.2 litres/ 2 pints
10 pints	4.5 litres/ 8 pints

Liquid measures

Imperial	ml	fl oz
1 teaspoon	5	
2 tablespoons	30	
4 tablespoons	60	
¼ pint/ 1 gill	150	5
⅓ pint	200	7
½ pint	300	10
¾ pint	425	15
1 pint	600	20
1¾ pints	1000 (1 litre)	35

Oven temperatures

American	Celsius	Fahrenheit	Gas Mark
Cool	130	250	½
Very slow	140	275	1
Slow	150	300	2
Moderate	160	320	3
Moderate	180	350	4
Moderately hot	190	375	5
Fairly hot	200	400	6
Hot	220	425	7
Very hot	230	450	8
Extremely hot	240	475	9

Other useful measurements

Measurement	Metric	Imperial
1 American cup	225 ml	8 fl oz
1 egg, size 3	50 ml	2 fl oz
1 egg white	30 ml	1 fl oz
1 rounded tablespoon flour	30 g	1 oz
1 rounded tablespoon cornflour	30 g	1 oz
1 rounded tablespoon caster sugar	30 g	1 oz
2 level teaspoons gelatine	10 g	¼ oz